D1422432

CYRIL LIGNAC

BISTRO COOKING

Le Chardenoux des Prés

"It is all a question of chance encounters, emotions and desires. I had this profound, sincere need to return to the source of my vocation and propose more traditional meals in a family like atmosphere. I wanted a place where people would enjoy getting together, amongst family or friends, to share conversations that would inspire neighbouring tables, and which would, by the sheer magic of the place, become one."

CYRIL LIGNAC

SCOTTISH BORDERS LIBRARY SERVICES	
008853232	
Bertrams	30/05/2013
641.594	£15.99

CYRIL LIGNAC

BISTRO COOKING

Le Chardenoux des Prés

Restaurant photographer: Arthur Delloye
Recipes photographer: Thomas Dhellemmes
Food stylist: Garlone Bardel

hachette
CUISINE

SCOTTISH BORDERS COUNCIL

Table of contents

After an apprenticeship in his native region of Aveyron in South Western, France, Cyril Lignac made his way to Paris in 2000 to work in the kitchen of L'Arpège, the famed restaurant of Chef Alain Passard. He continued to hone his skills alongside top chefs, namely the Pourcel brothers at La Maison Blanche and Le Jardin des Sens. By 2005, 5 million people were following Cyril Lignac on TV as he opened his own restaurant, Le Quinzième, on the popular French series "Oui Chef!". Here he brilliantly demonstrated his know-how and good taste, producing refined and slightly off-beat cooking, always made with his trademark top quality ingredients.

Cyril's generous, friendly and down to earth personality came to life through the chef 's TV programs and cook-books. His personal style truly changed the rules of the game in French households. For the first time, a French chef was telling people it was ok to mess up in their home kitchens. Thanks to him, cooking became fun and accessible for all, as opposed to a strict discipline driven by rules and highly technical step-by-step recipes. In 2008, Cyril made history when he took over Le Chardenoux, one of the last true Parisian bistros in existence. His menu gave a new pride of place to French specialties, enhancing them with fresh meaning, thanks to the chef 's own modern touches. This was seasonal bistro-style cooking made with ingredients from the finest producers and craftsmen, and intended for tables full of friends in a convivial and relaxed atmosphere.

In 2010, in his passion for reaching an ever wider audience, the Chef opened his workshop, Cuisine Attitude. In short, a place for culinary creation welcoming both novices and budding amateur chefs in the very center of Paris. In 2011, he brought the Chardenoux bistro concept to a new venue in the ever so Parisian Saint-Germain des Prés when he took over the legendary Claude Sainlouis renaming it Le Chardenoux des Prés. That same year, Cyril Lignac also opened La Pâtisserie, a simple though elegant bakery focusing on tradition, with a modern touch. In 2012, Cyril Lignac received his first Michelin star for his gourmet restaurant Le Quinzième. At the same time, GQ Magazine recognized his entrepreneurial spirit and his talent for sharing simple pleasures when they named him "Chef of the Year".

LE CHARDENOUX DES PRÉS

Ever driven by his quest for authenticity, he has created a site steeped in history. His search led him to the Claude Sainlouis, the "not-to- be-missed" Saint-Germain des Prés restaurant in vogue in the 1960/70s. While preserving the location's original spirit, he named it Le Chardenoux des Prés, echoing his first bistro on the Rue Jules Vallès. The celebrated original floral tapestry has been restored, along with the original mustard-coloured stoneware tiles which blend beautifully with the camel hue of the leather banquettes. The clothed tables are lit with vintage 1950s lamps and the marble bar has been enlarged to offer more comfort and space.

Starters

Carpaccio of sea bream flavoured with citrus and Espelette chilli pepper

PREPARATION TIME: 30 MINUTES   FOR 4 PEOPLE

• Rinse the two sea bream fillets under running fresh water. Lay them on a damp cloth and refrigerate.

• Cut four 15cm squares of greaseproof paper. Spread them out in front of you and place a 12cm cooking ring on one of the sheets. Cut the sea bream fillets in two lengthways, then slice them thinly. Place the thin slices of sea bream within the ring, so that they overlap slightly. Remove the ring and do the same on the other three sheets of greaseproof paper. Cover each carpaccio with cling film and refrigerate.

• Pour the juice and zest of the lime into a salad bowl and add the white balsamic vinegar. Mix together and add the olive oil. Season with fine salt and put this vinaigrette aside in a cool place until ready to serve.

• Using a pastry brush, baste the carpaccio with the lime vinaigrette. Turn the sea bream carpaccios out on to cold plates and baste the other side with the vinaigrette in the same way. Use a zester to grate the citrus fruit zests, and sprinkle over the carpaccios. Finish with a few sprigs of dill and sprinkle over the fleur de sel de Guérande and Espelette chilli powder. Serve.

2 gilthead sea bream fillets
(400g each)
———
Juice and finely grated zest of
1 unwaxed lime
5cl white balsamic vinegar
10cl olive oil
Fine salt
———
Zest of 1 unwaxed lime
Zest of 1 unwaxed lemon
Zest of 1 unwaxed orange
A few sprigs of dill
Pinch of fleur de sel de Guérande
Pinch of ground Espelette chilli pepper

Light lemongrass and ginger broth, with cubes of fresh foie gras

PREPARATION THE DAY BEFORE: 3 HOURS

PREPARATION TIME: 30 MINUTES   COOKING TIME: 1 HOUR 10   FOR 4 PEOPLE

• The night before, peel the carrot and onion, then wash the leek. Chop everything finely to prepare a bouquet garni. Place the whole chicken in a large pot or casserole dish. Cover completely with cold water and add the rock salt. Bring to the boil. After 1 or 2 minute(s), skim off the scum that has risen to the surface using a slotted spoon. Reduce the heat to simmering point and add the bouquet garni, pepper, peeled ginger, clove, bay leaf and thyme. Leave to simmer for 2½ hours. Once cooked, strain the broth using a fine sieve. Let it cool, then stand overnight in the fridge. You can use the chicken for another dish, such as a Caesar salad.

• The next day, use a spoon to remove the layer of fat that will have formed on the surface of the broth. Then pour the broth into a frying pan. Heat the broth, adding the tied bunch of coriander and the lemon grass, which should be cut in half lengthways. Leave to infuse for 1 hour, then remove the coriander and lemon grass and correct the seasoning for salt. Remove from the heat and set aside.

• Cut the foie gras into 1.5cm cubes by using a sharp knife which, dipped regularly into hot water, will help you cut cleanly. Place the cubes on a plate, cover with cling film and set aside in the fridge. Slice the mushrooms in half and then diagonally.

• 10 minutes before serving, remove the foie gras cubes from the fridge. Place the shiitake mushroom pieces in four soup dishes. Season the foie gras with salt and drop the cubes briefly into a little hot broth in order to cook them lightly. Drain and place the cubes in the soup dishes alongside the shiitake mushrooms. Pour over the hot broth. Give a twist of black pepper over each plate, then decorate with a few mini-coriander leaves.

1 carrot
1 onion
The green leaves of 1 leek
1 whole chicken
10g rock salt
5 peppercorns
15g fresh ginger
1 clove
½ bay leaf
1 sprig of thyme
½ bunch of coriander
1 stick of lemongrass
Fine salt

―――――

4 fillets of fresh foie gras (50g each)
8 shiitake mushrooms
A few baby coriander leaves
Fine salt and freshly milled pepper

Shredded crab
with warm potato salad

PREPARATION TIME: 35 MINUTES   COOKING TIME: 35 MINUTES   FOR 4 PEOPLE

• Fill a large saucepan with enough water to cover the crabs. Add the herbs (clove, pepper, thyme, bay leaf) and the rock salt. Bring to the boil. Drop the crabs into the pan and leave them to cook for 25 to 30 minutes. Once cooked, turn off the heat and drain the crabs. Leave them to cool on a plate before shelling. Put the crab meat aside in the fridge.

• Peel and rinse the potatoes and place in a pan of cold salted water. Bring to the boil. Cook until soft. Once cooked, drain and leave to one side.

• Prepare a vinaigrette in a salad bowl by mixing the mayonnaise with the balsamic vinegar and water. Season with salt and freshly milled pepper. Put to one side.

• Finely chop the leaves of the little gem lettuce, then add to the crab meat along with the finely-chopped chives. Season with the vinaigrette, salt and pepper.

• Slice the cherry tomatoes finely and place to one side in a cool place. Cut the warm potatoes into small pieces and season with the vinaigrette.

• Place an 8cm cooking ring on to each dinner plate. Put a spoonful of potato into each ring and press down gently. Then add a little of the crab and lettuce mixture. Decorate the top with the slices of cherry tomato, letting them overlap slightly. Season with Guérande sea salt. Place a sprig of chervil on each tower and decorate the plate with a few drops of vinaigrette. Lift off the ring before serving.

2 crabs (800g each)
1 clove
10 black peppercorns
1 sprig of thyme
½ bay leaf
10g rock salt
1 little gem lettuce
1 bunch of chives
Pinch of fine salt
A twist of freshly milled pepper

———

6 small Ratte potatoes
10g rock salt

———

50g home-made mayonnaise
A dash of white balsamic vinegar
10cl water
Pinch of fine salt
A twist of freshly milled pepper

———

15 cherry tomatoes
Fleur de sel de Guérande
4 sprigs of chervil

The Chardenoux des Prés Croque-Monsieur

PREPARATION TIME: 20 MINUTES

COOKING TIME: 15 MINUTES   REFRIGERATION: 8 HOURS   FOR 4 PEOPLE

• Cut the crusts off the bread and then cut into five slices lengthways. Melt the butter over a low heat in a frying pan. Place the slices of bread on a baking tray, soak both sides in the butter using a pastry brush, using about three quarters of the butter.

• Cut the ham slices to fit the bread. Cover each slice of bread with cold béchamel sauce. Place a slice of ham on each of the four slices of bread, then add a slice of Comté cheese and finally a second slice of ham.

• Place the garnished bread slices one on top of the other and the final one upside down to close the croque-monsieur sandwich. Wrap it fairly tightly in cling film. Put in the fridge for 8 hours, until firm.

• Preheat the oven to 180°C (350°F, gas mark 6). Unwrap the croque-monsieur and cut it into four thick slices. Place these on a baking tray and baste with the rest of the melted butter. Sprinkle over the grated Parmesan cheese. Put the croque-monsieur slices in the oven for 8 minutes, then turn the oven to grill and leave until the top has just browned.

• Serve each croque-monsieur with a side salad seasoned with vinaigrette.

1 small white sandwich loaf
(15cm x 9cm x 8cm)
150g unsalted butter
8 slices of ham (3mm thick)
150g Béchamel sauce
4 slices of Comté cheese
(15cm x 9cm and 3mm thick)
100g grated Parmesan cheese
4 bunches of salad
1 dash of vinaigrette made with
white balsamic vinegar and olive oil
(see p. 76)

Smoked foie gras terrine
with rhubarb and ginger chutney

PREPARATION THE DAY BEFORE: 30 MINUTES + 24 HOURS RESTING TIME
PREPARATION ON THE DAY: 3 HOURS 15   COOKING TIME: 1 HOUR   FOR 4 PEOPLE

• The day before, place the foie gras on a sheet of greaseproof paper and carefully remove the nerve. Put it on a plate and then into the cold smoking oven for 30 minutes. At the end of the smoking cycle, remove the foie gras and season with the salt, pepper, sugar, port and cognac. Place the fillet in a terrine and cover with cling film. Leave to rest for 12 hours.

• Preheat the oven to 100°C (210°F gas mark 3-4). Remove the cling film from the terrine and place in a deep dish. Pour boiling water around the terrine. Place this bain-marie in the oven and leave to cook for 1 hour. Once cooked, remove the bain-marie from the oven and remove the terrine. Place on a clean plate and cover with a sheet of greaseproof paper. Place two cartons of milk (2 litres) on top to create a press. The fat will run out from the edges of the terrine. Place in the fridge for 12 hours.

• The following day, remove the press and scrape off the fat that has run out around the foie gras. Melt it gently in a small saucepan, then filter it through a clean muslin cloth. Pour this fat back over the terrine and place back in the fridge for 2½ hours.

• Put the water, sugar and grenadine syrup in a saucepan and bring to the boil. Turn off the heat and allow to cool for 10 minutes. Drop the ribbons of rhubarb into this syrup, cover the pan and leave to infuse for 10 minutes. Then drain the rhubarb and leave it on a plate in a cool place.

• In the meantime, place the butter in a frying pan. Peel and finely chop the ginger and add this to the pan. Cook on a very low heat for 5 minutes, then chop the remaining rhubarb finely and add this to the pan. Cook for a few more minutes, then sprinkle over the sugar and continue to cook for another 20 minutes. The mixture should have thickened to form a marmalade. Leave aside to cool.

• Bring a saucepan of water to the boil and dip a sharp knife into it. Use this to un-mould the foie gras from the terrine, then cut it into slices of 50g. Place each slice on a dinner plate. Sprinkle over the fleur de sel de Guérande and the freshly milled pepper. Place a little spoonful of rhubarb chutney next to each slice, roll up the ribbons of rhubarb and place three on each plate next to the chutney, with a sprig of chervil on each roll. Add a few drops of the rhubarb cooking syrup, having reduced it slightly first. Serve with a slice of toasted sourdough.

1 duck foie gras fillet (650g)
8g fine salt
Pinch of ground pepper (1g)
Pinch of caster sugar (1g)
32cl port
32cl cognac

———

50cl water
125g caster sugar
2cl grenadine syrup
12 fine ribbons of rhubarb
(2mm thick)

———

15g unsalted butter
20g fresh ginger
250g rhubarb
50g caster sugar

———

Fleur de sel de Guérande
A twist of freshly milled pepper
4 sprigs of chervil
4 slices of sourdough bread

Brocciu and chard macaroni gratin with mature parmesan and meat jus

PREPARATION TIME: 35 MINUTES   COOKING TIME: 35 MINUTES   FOR 4 PEOPLE

• Fill a saucepan with enough water to cook the macaroni. Add the coarse salt to the water. Bring to the boil, then lower the heat until just simmering. Drop the macaroni into the water and cook for 7 minutes. Once cooked, drain carefully without refreshing them. Baste immediately with olive oil using a pastry brush. Cover a tray with cling film and place onto it the macaroni, which should be cut into four. Put aside in a cool place. Remove the Swiss chard leaves with a knife. Drop them into a large saucepan of boiling salted water and cook until soft. Drain and refresh them in a bowl of iced water. Squeeze them lightly with your hands, then chop into small pieces. Put aside in a cool place.

• Use a vegetable peeler to peel the chard stems and chop finely. Pour the oil into a hot frying pan and add the slightly salted butter. Let it melt before adding the chopped chard. Season with salt and pour in the chicken stock. Cook until the pieces of chard are nice and tender. Then use a slotted spoon to drain them and set aside in a cool place. Mix the green and white parts of the cooled chard with the Brocciu cheese in a salad bowl. Add the finely chopped basil and season with salt and freshly milled black pepper. Stuff the macaroni with this mixture. Place them snugly, four by four, in a baking tray.

• Heat the cream in a small saucepan and let it reduce by half. Then remove from the heat and stir in the grated parmesan. Set aside at room temperature.

• Put the milk and remaining cream in another saucepan. Bring to the boil and reduce by a quarter. Add the remaining grated parmesan. Mix with a hand blender to obtain a nice mousse. If the mousse doesn't hold, try adding a little more full fat milk and mixing again.

• Cover the macaroni with the cream and parmesan mixture. Turn the oven to grill and put in the baking sheet. Leave until nicely brown. After cooking, place 4 macaroni in the centre of each dinner plate. Pour the parmesan mousse on one side and the reheated meat jus on the other. Decorate each plate with a basil leaf.

4 large pieces of macaroni
(50cm in length by 1.5cm in diameter)
5g coarse Guérande sea salt
5cl olive oil

----

1 large Swiss chard
5g coarse Guérande sea salt
5cl olive oil
15g slightly salted butter
10cl chicken stock
200g Brocciu (a Corsican cheese)
½ bunch of basil
Salt and freshly-milled black pepper

50cl double cream
50g grated, organic "La Villa" parmesan

25cl full fat milk`
25cl double cream
100g grated, organic "La Villa" parmesan

15cl meat jus
4 basil leaves

Curried shellfish velouté with wakamé

PREPARATION TIME: 30 MINUTES   COOKING TIME: 35 MINUTES   FOR 4 PEOPLE

• Wash and clean the mussels. Put sixteen aside in a cool place. Melt the butter in a large saucepan. Add the chopped shallots and the mussels. Stir and deglaze with the white wine. Add the thyme, bay leaf, pepper and water. Cover and cook for 5 minutes on a high heat. Take the saucepan off the heat and drain the mussels. Sieve the juice from the mussels through a muslin cloth and pour into a second saucepan. Shell the mussels and put them in a cool place. Discard the shells.

• Add the cream and the wakamé to the mussel juice, then boil for 10 minutes. Next add the curry powder and simmer for another 10 minutes. Add the cooked mussels and heat for 5 minutes. Use a mixer to purée the mixture then strain through a conical strainer or fine sieve. Pour the resulting mixture into another saucepan. Add the mashed potato and mix again. Put this velouté to one side.

• Open the clams at the last minute and the sixteen remaining mussels. Shell eight clams and twelve mussels, keeping four of each in their shells.

• Place six potato slices in each soup dish. Spread among them the mussels and clams, with and without shells, the bread croutons and the sprigs of chickweed (or other salad leaves), as shown opposite. Pour the hot mussel and wakamé velouté into the middle and around the edges of each dish.

1kg Bouchot mussels
15g unsalted butter
2 shallots
10cl dry white wine
2 sprigs of thyme
1 large bay leaf
10 black peppercorns
20cl water
75cl double cream
50g rehydrated wakamé
(an edible seaweed)
3g curry powder
100g mashed potatoes
500g clams

24 slices (2cm in diameter) of boiled
Ratte potatoes
12 croutons
16 sprigs of chickweed
(or other green salad leaf)

Burrata with Ligurian olive oil and grilled vegetables

PREPARATION TIME: 30 MINUTES   COOKING TIME: 40 MINUTES   FOR 4 PEOPLE

• Drain the burrata, dry them gently and place in a dish. Pour over the Ligurian olive oil. Keep refrigerated.

Cook the spring onions in salted boiling water, then refresh in iced water. Split the green asparagus and the artichokes in half lengthways.

• Bring a saucepan of water to the boil. Drop in the tomatoes for 30 seconds, then peel them. Cut into four, take out the seeds and put to one side. Fry the skins in a little olive oil (2cl). Put the fried skins to one side on a plate covered with kitchen paper.

• Preheat the oven to 180°C (350°F, gas mark 6). Place the peppers on a sheet of aluminium foil. Pour over 10cl of olive oil, a pinch of salt and the thyme. Close the foil to make a parcel and put in the oven to cook for 35 minutes. Once cooked, remove the peppers, skin them and cut into four. Using a 4cm cutter, cut four circles from each pepper. Keep to one side.

• Trickle the last of the olive oil on to a griddle, then lay on the courgette slices, the circles of pepper, asparagus, onions, artichokes and aubergine slices. Brown all the vegetables on both sides. Use the same cutter to make circles of aubergine, as you did for the pepper.

• In each serving dish, arrange the vegetable discs in a spiral. Put the burrata in the centre, then place the asparagus, onions and artichokes attractively around the edges. Add the tomato quarters and the fried skins. Decorate with some basil leaves. Season the burrata with fleur de sel and freshly milled pepper. Serve.

4 burrata (Italian cheese)
10cl Ligurian extra virgin olive oil
4 spring onions
4 green asparagus
4 purple artichokes
3 vine tomatoes
14cl olive oil
1 yellow pepper
1 red pepper
Pinch of salt
2 sprigs of thyme
8 slices of courgette
4 slices of aubergine
12 basil leaves
4 pinches of fleur de sel de Guérande
4 twists of freshly milled pepper

Warm green asparagus from Landes, with sauce mousseline and a lime and herb vinaigrette

PREPARATION TIME: 30 MINUTES   COOKING TIME: 20 MINUTES   FOR 4 PEOPLE

• Put the water, white vinegar, ground pepper and salt in a small saucepan. Reduce by three quarters before adding the egg yolks. Mix with a wire whisk until nicely frothy. Trickle in the hot clarified butter, while still stirring. Season with salt and the lemon juice. Put this hollandaise sauce to one side and keep warm in a bain-marie.

• Pour the balsamic vinegar and the olive oil into a salad bowl. Season with salt and add the finely chopped herbs and the lime zest – grate this with a Microplane® grater. Leave the vinaigrette to one side.

• Using a small knife, remove the small leaves from the asparagus stems, leaving those at the tip, then cut each stem to 12cm long. Next, peel and slightly cut away 2cm from the tail end. Bring a large pan of salted water to the boil. Drop in the asparagus and cook for 7 minutes. Then place the asparagus on kitchen paper before brushing with olive oil to make them glisten. Tuck the asparagus into a white cloth. Add the whipped cream to the hollandaise sauce and mix carefully. Serve the asparagus with this sauce mousseline and the herb vinaigrette.

5 tablespoons water
2 tablespoons white vinegar
Pinch of coarse ground pepper
5 egg yolks
350g clarified butter
Juice of half a lemon
4 tablespoons whipped cream
Fine salt

————

3cl white balsamic vinegar
9cl extra virgin olive oil
Pinch of salt
A sprig of coriander
A sprig of tarragon
6 chives
Zest of 2 unwaxed limes

————

16 green asparagus from Landes
5g coarse Guérande sea salt
2cl extra virgin olive oil

White asparagus and lamb's lettuce salad, with soft boiled egg and shavings of mimolette cheese

PREPARATION TIME: 30 MINUTES   COOKING TIME: 15 MINUTES   FOR 4 PEOPLE

• Bring a large saucepan of water to the boil, then carefully lower the eggs into the boiling liquid. Cook for 6 minutes. Remove the eggs and cool in a bowl of iced water. Shell the eggs and put to one side in a cool place.

• Using a small knife, remove the tiny leaves from the asparagus stem – leave those on the tips - then cut them to 12cm long. Bring a large saucepan of salted water to the boil. Drop in the asparagus and cook for 8 minutes. Drain and refresh in iced water. Drain again, then cut into fine slices of 0.5cm thickness. Leave the tips whole, at 5cm in length.

• Put a frying pan over a low heat, add the butter, the chicken stock and the asparagus. Season with the fine salt.

• Lower the eggs into a saucepan of hot water for 4 minutes to reheat them. Drain and dry with a piece of kitchen towel, then sprinkle over the fleur de sel and the freshly milled pepper.

• Mix the lamb's lettuce in a salad bowl with the vinaigrette made from white balsamic vinegar and olive oil. Season with fine salt, then share the lamb's lettuce between four glass bowls. Place the asparagus carefully among the salad leaves, then place the warm eggs in the middle of each bowl. Finish with the shavings of mimolette and serve immediately.

4 very fresh eggs
A pinch of fleur de sel de Guérande
Freshly milled pepper

---

12 white asparagus
5g Guérande sea salt
1 tablespoon slightly salted butter
1 tablespoon chicken stock
Pinch of fine salt

---

4 bunches of lamb's lettuce
1 splash of vinaigrette made with white balsamic vinegar and olive oil (see p. 76)
24 fine shavings of mature mimolette cheese
Fine salt

Main dishes

Griddled scallops with white asparagus and a creamy orange sauce

PREPARATION TIME: 1 HOUR   COOKING TIME: 25 MINUTES   FOR 4 PEOPLE

• Remove the scallops from their shells and clean them (or ask your fishmonger to do this for you). Place the scallops on kitchen paper and keep in a cool place. Wash the beards under cold running water, then drain.

• Pour a dash of olive oil into a frying pan or saucepan. Heat and then add the scallop beards. Stir and allow the water to seep out. Cook until all the liquid has reduced. Add the salted butter, stir and add the peeled and chopped shallot. Cook for a few minutes until nicely browned then add the peeled and quartered orange.. Continue to brown until nicely caramelized. Pour in the cream, bring to the boil, then lower the heat and leave to cook for 20 minutes. When cooked, sieve the sauce, squeezing out all the juices from the scallop beards. Cut the unsalted butter into small cubes and add to the sauce, then whisk together using a hand blender. Check for seasoning, adding a little fine salt if necessary. Remove from the heat and set aside.

• Peel the white asparagus and cut to a length of 12cm from the tip. Cook them in a large saucepan of boiling salted water for seven minutes per kilo for calibre 22 asparagus. To check whether they are cooked, pierce an asparagus spear with the blade of a knife: it should go in and be removed easily. When cooked, drain the asparagus and plunge into a basin of iced water. As soon as they are cold, drain them again quickly to avoid them taking in too much water. Place on to kitchen paper and keep cold.

• Season the scallops with fine salt. Drizzle olive oil on a griddle and place the scallops flat-side down on to it. Brown quickly, then remove to an ovenproof dish, coloured side down. Reheat the asparagus in a saucepan or frying pan with a knob of salted butter and the chicken stock. Turn the oven to grill and place the scallops under the grill for three minutes. Then lay them on kitchen paper and sprinkle with fleur de sel de Guérande.

• Place three asparagus on each dinner plate, then five scallops on top. Decorate with the orange segments and the basil leaves. Use a hand blender to whisk up the orange sauce into a foam and add a little to each plate. Serve the rest of the creamy orange sauce on the side.

20 large scallops
A dash of olive oil for cooking
Fine salt
Fleur de sel de Guérande

———

A dash of olive oil
10g slightly salted butter
1 shallot
1 orange
500g double cream
150g cold unsalted butter
Pinch of fine salt

———

12 white Landes asparagus spears
5g coarse Guérande sea salt
A knob of slightly salted butter
15cl chicken stock

———

12 orange segments, peeled
12 basil leaves

Oven-baked Breton sea bass, with a carrot and turmeric purée

PREPARATION THE DAY BEFORE: 35 MINUTES + 1 RESTING OVERNIGHT
PREPARATION ON THE DAY: 35 MINUTES   COOKING TIME: 15 MINUTES   FOR 4 PEOPLE

• The night before, rinse the fish under cold running water, clean, scale and gut it (or ask your fishmonger to do this for you). Fillet the sea bass, leaving the skin on. Place the two fillets on a flat plate, sprinkle with coarse salt and caster sugar, and leave to marinate in the fridge for 10 minutes. Rinse the fillets under cold running water and remove the bones. Wrap the fillets in a clean cloth for 20 minutes to dry them, then change the cloth and leave them in the fridge overnight.

• The next day, trim the fillets, still leaving the skin on. Put the two fillets together head to tail and roll them up, making sure the skin is on the outside of the roll. Wrap the roll in cling film and put it in the freezer for 20 minutes, then cut into 110g portions. Refrigerate.

• Put the chicken stock, slightly salted butter, a dash of olive oil, thyme, bay leaf and peeled garlic together in a sauté pan.
Peel the young carrots, keeping 1cm of their green tops. Drop them into a saucepan of salted boiling water and cook for seven minutes. Drain and refresh in iced water. Leave aside on kitchen paper in a cool place.

• Peel the carrots and chop into round slices. Drop them into a saucepan of salted boiling water and cook until nice and tender. Once cooked, drain and place in the bowl of a Thermomix® or a vegetable mouli (mill). Add the butter, cut into small cubes, and the turmeric. Mix until smooth and add salt to taste. Put to one side.

• Pour the carrot, orange and ginger juices into a saucepan. Reduce by a quarter before adding the cream. Reduce again and whisk in the cubes of butter. Salt to taste.

• Place the sea bass fillets in the thyme stock. Simmer for 10 minutes, basting regularly. Turn them over and baste once more. Drain on kitchen paper. Use scissors to snip away the cling film.

• Arrange a spoonful of carrot purée in a tear shape on each plate. Glaze the young carrots with melted butter using a pastry brush, and add three to each plate. Place a piece of sea bass on the other side of each plate. Use a hand-blender to emulsify the sauce and place a spoonful on each plate. Decorate with chervil.

1 Breton sea bass (2kg)
200g coarse Guérande sea salt
100g caster sugar
_____

50cl chicken stock
5g slightly salted butter
A dash of olive oil
1 sprig of thyme
1 small bay leaf
1 clove of garlic
_____

12 young carrots with their leaves
5g coarse Guérande sea salt
10g cold slightly salted butter
_____

500g carrots
5g coarse Guérande sea salt
75g cold unsalted butter
3g powdered turmeric
Pinch of fine salt
_____

400g carrot juice
200g orange juice
50g ginger juice
350g double cream
75g cold unsalted butter
Pinch of fine salt
_____

4 sprigs of chervil

Monkfish with tandoori spices, smooth parsnip purée and creamy sesame sauce

PREPARATION THE DAY BEFORE: 35 MINUTES + 1 RESTING OVERNIGHT
PREPARATION TIME: 35 MINUTES   COOKING TIME: 15 MINUTES   FOR 4 PEOPLE

• The night before, rinse the monkfish under cold running water, clean, gut and fillet it (or ask the fishmonger to do this for you). Place the fillets on a flat plate, sprinkle with coarse salt and caster sugar and leave in the fridge to marinate for 10 minutes. Rinse the monkfish fillets under cold running water before removing the bones. Wrap the fillets in a clean cloth for 20 minutes to dry them, then change the cloth and leave overnight in the refrigerator.

• The next day, cut the fillets into 110g pieces. Wrap tightly in cling film to make an airtight parcel. Keep cool.

Peel the parsnips and cut into round slices. Pour the milk and cream into a saucepan and drop in the parsnips. Season with fine salt. Cook for 20 to 30 minutes. When cooked, drain the parsnips and mix them with the cubed butter and a little of the cooking juice. Season with salt. Put this mixture to one side.

• Heat a dash of olive oil and 10g butter in a saucepan. Let it colour slightly before adding the chopped onions, sesame and bean sprouts. Cook for 10 minutes, then pour in the cream and cook for another 30 minutes. Stir the sauce and put it through a fine sieve. Whisk in the remaining cubes of butter (50g), salt to taste and set aside.

• Put the pieces of monkfish, still in their airtight packages, into the thermoplongeur (machine for sous vide cooking), set to 52.2°C (126°F) for 8 minutes. When the monkfish is cooked, lift it out and remove the cling film. Dry the pieces of monkfish then roll in a mixture of tandoori spices and sesame seeds, which have previously been toasted (in a dry frying pan). Slice each piece of fish into three.

• Place a spoonful of parsnip purée on each plate and arrange three pieces of monkfish beside it. Decorate with the bean sprouts and sprigs of chervil. Use a hand blender to emulsify the sauce and put a spoonful of the foam beside the fish.

1 monkfish (2kg)
200g coarse Guérande sea salt
100g caster sugar
50g powdered tandoori spices
150g white sesame seeds

____

500g parsnips
25cl full fat milk
500g double cream
75g cold unsalted butter
Fine salt

____

A dash of olive oil
60g unsalted butter
1 bunch of spring onions
100g white sesame seeds
150g fresh bean sprouts
50cl single cream
Pinch of fine salt

____

12 fresh bean sprouts
12 sprigs of chervil

Cod cooked in white wine, smoked potatoes and a buttery mussel sauce

PREPARATION THE DAY BEFORE: 2 HOURS 30 + 1 RESTING OVERNIGHT

PREPARATION TIME: 35 MINUTES   COOKING TIME: 25 MINUTES   FOR 4 PEOPLE

• The night before, fillet the cod (or ask your fishmonger to do this for you). Remove the skin. Put the fillets on a flat plate, sprinkle with the coarse sea salt and sugar, then leave in the fridge to marinate for 10 minutes. Rinse them under cold running water and remove the bones. Leave the fillets wrapped in a clean cloth for 20 minutes to dry them, then change the cloth and leave in the fridge overnight.

• Peel the onion, slice into small quarters and separate out the petals. Pour the red and white wines into a saucepan. Bring to the boil, then lower the heat and drop in the petals of onion. Cook until tender. Cover with cling film and leave overnight in the cooking juices.

• The next day, place the two cod fillets head to tail and roll them up in cling film to form a roll. Place in the freezer for 20 minutes, then cut into 110g pieces.

• Clean the mussels then put them in a saucepan with a dash of olive oil. Add the thyme, bay leaf, peeled garlic, clove and peppercorns. Deglaze with the white wine and water, then cover and cook until the mussels open. Put the mussels in their shells in a large bowl covered with cling film and keep in a cool place. Sieve the mussel jus through a fine cloth.

• Use a parisienne scoop (melon baller) to cut out small balls of potato. Rinse the potato balls in cold water and dry them. Heat a dash of olive oil and the butter in a frying pan. Add the potato balls and roll them around to coat them in the butter. Pour in 250g of the mussel jus and leave to cook until the potatoes are tender. Drain them into a dish and place in a smoking oven for 20 minutes. Keep to one side. If you don't have a smoking oven, heat up some dry thyme and rosemary in a large saucepan. Place the dish of potatoes inside and cover with a lid.

• Pour 75g of mussel jus, the Noilly Prat and the cream into a sauté pan. Bring to the boil and reduce by half. Use a hand blender to whisk up the sauce. Remove from the heat and put aside.

• Put a piece of cod, a few potato balls and some mussels in each small casserole dish. Add the onion petals and the spinach leaves (brush these with oil first). Use a hand blender to froth up the Noilly Prat sauce and pour a little into each dish.

1 cod (1-2kg)
200g coarse Guérande sea salt
100g caster sugar

_____

1 red onion
5cl white wine
5cl red wine

_____

A dash of olive oil
450g Bouchot mussels
1 sprig of thyme
1 small bay leaf
1 clove of garlic
1 clove
10 peppercorns
15cl dry white wine
25cl water

_____

3 charlotte potatoes
A dash of olive oil
15g slightly salted butter
250g jus from the mussels

_____

75g jus from the mussels
125g vermouth (Noilly Prat)
300g single cream
50g cold unsalted butter

_____

12 baby spinach leaves
A dash of olive oil

White fish cooked in brown butter, with pasta shells and ham

PREPARATION TIME: 45 MINUTES   COOKING TIME: 15 MINUTES   FOR 4 PEOPLE

• Pour a dash of olive oil into a saucepan and add the butter. Add the pasta shells, season with fine salt and moisten with chicken stock. Simmer gently for 10 minutes. Once cooked, put to one side.

• Pour the milk and cream into a second saucepan. Reduce by half before adding the grated parmesan. Cook again until thick and creamy, then place in a bain-marie to keep warm.

• Pour a dash of olive oil into a sauté pan and add the butter. Let it brown slightly before adding the white fish fillets, skin-side down. Press down lightly with your fingers so that the fillets remain nice and flat. Baste with the foaming butter and turn them over. Cook for 10 minutes, or until the centre of each fillet is hot. You can test this by pricking the fillet with a toothpick. Place the toothpick in the palm of your hand - it should feel nice and hot. Once cooked, remove the fillets from the pan and place on kitchen paper, skin-side up. Sprinkle with fleur de sel.

• Brown the slices of ham quickly on the griddle or in a frying pan. Mix the pasta shells with the reduced cream and the cubes of ham. Check the seasoning for salt. Heat the creamy parmesan sauce: if too thick, thin with a little full fat milk.

• Place a little of the pasta shell mixture in the bottom of each "cocotte" (individual casserole dish) and place the white fish fillets on top. Decorate with a square of ham and a sprig of chervil, then finish with a spoonful of the parmesan sauce which you should emulsify beforehand with a hand blender.

A dash of olive oil
10g slightly salted butter
250g small pasta shells (coquillettes)
50cl chicken stock
Fine salt

———

250g single cream
100g full fat milk
50g grated parmesan

———

A dash of olive oil
15g slightly salted butter
4 pieces of lean white fish cut from the widest part of the fillet (110g each)
Fleur de sel de Guérande

———

4 slices of ham
1 tablespoon double cream, reduced
15g cooked ham in cubes
4 sprigs of chervil
Fine salt

Poached Breton lobster, rigatoni with lobster jus and basil

PREPARATION TIME: 1 HOUR   COOKING TIME: 40 MINUTES   FOR 4 PEOPLE

• Break the lobsters in half, keep the heads and pincers to make the sauce. Keep the coral if they have one. Remove the guts by making a slight incision in the stomach. Prick the length of the body with a wooden toothpick so that the tail lies flat. Place the lobster bodies in the freezer for 20 minutes. Take them out and wait 10 minutes before shelling them raw. Place in airtight bags and cook in a thermoplongeur (machine for sous vide cooking) at 60°C (140°F), for 8 minutes. Once cooked, refresh in a bowl of iced water.

• Heat a dash of olive oil in a pot. Add the lobster heads and pincers and crush them with a rolling pin. Leave on a medium heat until slightly caramelized. Add the bouquet garni and stir until slightly browned. Pour over the cognac and allow to reduce over a high heat until the liquid is absorbed with the cooking juices. Deglaze with the white wine and allow to reduce again. Add the tomato purée and the tomato, cut into quarters. Pour in the cream. Leave to simmer for 40 minutes.

• Sieve the sauce into a second pan, using a fine sieve. Reduce down until the sauce has a smooth, creamy consistency. Add the lobster corals and mix with a hand blender. Check the seasoning for salt.

• Put a dash of olive oil into a saucepan, followed by the pasta, season with salt and stir. Pour in the chicken stock and cook for eight minutes, until slightly firm, then remove from the cooking liquid.

• Reheat the lobster tails in the thermoplongeur (machine for sous vide cooking) for 15 minutes at 52.2°C (126°F). Put the clams in a small saucepan with a spoonful of water on a medium heat. Leave until they have opened. Brown the slightly salted butter in a sauté pan. Remove the lobsters from their packaging and flash fry them in the brown butter, then cut each tail into five thick slices.

• Reheat the pasta in the lobster sauce and arrange in glass dishes. Place the lobster slices on top, then decorate with the parmesan shavings, the basil leaves and the clams.

4 Breton lobsters (550g each)
A dash of virgin olive oil
1 bouquet garni (½ carrot, ½ onion, 1 stick of celery, a stick of leek)
5cl cognac
10cl white wine
1 tablespoon of tomato purée
1 tomato
75cl double cream
Fine salt

———

1 packet of rigatoni (500g)
A dash of olive oil
Pinch of fine salt
25cl chicken stock

———

16 clams
15g slightly salted butter
12 parmesan shavings
½ a bunch of basil

Griddled John Dory, tender green peas with Bellota chorizo

PREPARATION TIME: 35 MINUTES   COOKING TIME: 15 MINUTES   FOR 2 PEOPLE

• Fillet the John Dory (or ask your fishmonger to do this for you). Try to keep the two large fillets attached and separate the small one. Score the edges and place on a flat plate. Sprinkle with coarse sea salt and caster sugar. Leave in the fridge for 4 minutes, then rinse under cold running water. Dry the fillets with kitchen paper then put them back in the fridge until ready to cook.

• Drop the peas into a large saucepan of boiling salted water and cook for six or seven minutes. Refresh in a basin of iced water. Keep cool.

• Pour a dash of olive oil on to a griddle and add the John Dory fillets. Brown each side. Cook until tender. When cooked, remove the fillets from the griddle and lay on kitchen paper. Sprinkle with fleur de sel de Guérande.

• Pour the chicken stock into a saucepan and bring to the boil. Add the butter and drop in the peas. Season with fine salt if necessary, then add the diced chorizo.

• Place the two large John Dory fillets on each plate, with the third one on top. Arrange the peas and chorizo around them. Add the chorizo slices and onion slices. Finish with a dash of hot veal jus.

2 pieces of John Dory
(600-800g each)
200g coarse Guérande sea salt
50g caster sugar
5cl olive oil
Fleur de sel de Guérande

———

300g petit pois
5g coarse Guérande sea salt
5cl chicken stock
15g unsalted butter
25g diced Bellota chorizo
Fine salt

———

4 thin slices of chorizo,
2cm in diameter
1 spring onion, finely sliced
10cl veal jus

Grilled red mullet, shellfish and saffron risotto, paella-style

PREPARATION TIME: 1 HOUR COOKING TIME: 1 HOUR FOR 4 PEOPLE

- Gut and scale the red mullet, rinse in cold water then fillet them (or ask the fishmonger to do this for you). Take out the bones and trim the fillets to make them even. Keep in the fridge.

- Pour a dash of olive oil into a saucepan and add the butter. Let it melt, then add the chopped shallot and leave it to sweat. Pour in the rice and stir until coated with butter. Season with fine salt and saffron. Pour in the wine and reduce down, then moisten with chicken stock. Cook for 18 minutes, gradually adding stock as it reduces. Remove from the heat and put aside.

- Put 5cl olive oil and 20g butter into a preheated saucepan. Add half the chopped shallots and leave them to sweat. Rinse the razor clams under cold running water and add them to the pan. Deglaze the saucepan with half the white wine. Add the sprig of thyme and half the bay leaf. Cover and simmer for three minutes. Drain the razor clams, then sieve the jus and pour it into a saucepan. Keep the razor clam shells and dice the flesh. Put aside in a cool place. Cook the cockles in the same way. Shell them and put aside in a cool place. Mix the jus from the cockles with the jus from the razor clams and reduce by a quarter. Add the chicken stock and the cream then mix with a hand blender, adding the remaining cubes of cold butter (75g). Season with salt and saffron. Place in a bain-marie to keep warm.

- Cook the beans and peas in boiling salted water. Dice the peppers and the chorizo. Chop the squid into small cubes and griddle them quickly. Season. Mix half the beans and peas with the squid and chorizo cubes in a large bowl. Season with balsamic vinegar, olive oil and fine salt. Fill the razor clam shells with this mixture. Turn the oven to grill. Reheat the cooked rice with the rest of the diced chorizo, the beans, peas and peppers. Pour over a ladle full of chicken stock to give it the consistency of a risotto. Check the seasoning.

- Place the seasoned red mullet fillets on an oiled baking tray. Trickle olive oil over the fillets and place the tray under the grill. When cooked, remove the fillets on to kitchen paper. Sprinkle with fleur de sel.

- Use a 7 or 8cm cooking ring to arrange the risotto in the centre of each hot plate. Remove the ring and place the red mullet fillets onto the risotto. Add two garnished razor clam shells. Decorate with coriander. Serve the sauce hot in a sauceboat.

4 red mullet (250-300g each)
5cl olive oil
Pinch of fine salt
Pinch of fleur de sel de Guérande

_____

A dash of olive oil
10g unsalted butter
1 shallot
150g carnaroli rice
Pinch of fine salt
Pinch of powdered saffron
3cl dry white wine
500g chicken stock

_____

5cl olive oil
95g unsalted butter
1 shallot
12 razor clams
60g white wine
2 sprigs of thyme
1 bay leaf
200g cockles
100g chicken stock
50g single cream
Pinch of powdered saffron
Pinch of table salt

_____

50g green beans
50g fresh petit pois
15g pimientos del piquillos (small red peppers)
15g chorizo
1 squid (200g)
A dash of white balsamic vinegar
A dash of olive oil
Fine salt

_____

A bunch of fresh coriander shoots

Pollack cooked slowly in vin jaune, with vanilla mashed potato

PREPARATION THE DAY BEFORE: 30 MINUTES + 1 RESTING OVERNIGHT
PREPARATION TIME: 35 MINUTES   COOKING TIME: 1 HOUR   FOR 4 PEOPLE

• The night before, scale and fillet the pollack (or ask your fishmonger to do this for you). Keep the bone and clean the fish thoroughly under cold running water. Put the fillets on a flat plate, sprinkle with coarse salt and sugar, then leave to marinate in the fridge for 10 minutes. Rinse the fillets under cold running water before removing the bones. Wrap the fillets in a clean cloth for 20 minutes to dry them, then change the cloth and leave in the fridge overnight. The next day, place the fillets head to tail then wrap them tightly in cling film to form a roll. Place the roll in the freezer for 20 minutes, then cut into 110g pieces per person.

• Pour a dash of olive oil into a saucepan. Add the chopped shallots and the mushrooms, which should be sliced in half and then again diagonally, and fry them lightly. Add the pollack backbone, cut into pieces, and cook until all the liquid is absorbed. Deglaze with white wine and reduce by three quarters, then pour in the cream and cook until the mixture just coats the back of a spoon. Sieve the sauce and then whisk in the cubes of butter with a hand blender. Add the vin jaune and cook for another 10 minutes.

• Peel the potatoes and rinse them. Drop them with the coarse salt into a saucepan of water and cook for 40 minutes. Split the vanilla pod in half lengthways and scrape out the insides with a knife to retrieve the flesh. Put the vanilla with the milk and a quarter of the butter cubes in a second saucepan. Place a vegetable mouli over this saucepan and purée the potatoes into the sauce. Stir well and add the rest of the cold butter. Once the purée is nice and smooth, add the salt.

• Heat the oven to 150°C (300°F, gas mark 5). Put the vin jaune, chicken stock, thyme, bay leaf and peeled garlic into an oven-proof dish. Heat for a few minutes, then add the pieces of pollack. Cook in the oven for 20 minutes. Once cooked, leave the fish to rest for a few minutes.

• Pour a dash of olive oil into a frying pan and add the baby spinach leaves (set aside the 12 prettiest for the garnish). Spear the peeled garlic with a fork and use this to stir the spinach. Season with fine salt and spread the spinach leaves in the bottom of each cocotte (individual casserole dish). Place the pollack on top, with a spoonful of the potato purée and the vin jaune sauce, emulsified beforehand with a hand blender. Decorate with the reserved spinach leaves. Serve with a side dish of purée and the rest of the sauce in a sauceboat.

1 pollack (1-2kg)
200g coarse Guérande sea salt
100g caster sugar
10cl vin jaune (a dry white wine from the Jura similar to fino sherry)
10cl chicken stock
1 sprig of thyme
1 small bay leaf
1 clove of garlic

———

A dash of olive oil
1 shallot
50g mushrooms
The backbone of the pollack
20cl white wine
75cl single cream
30g unsalted butter
50g vin jaune

———

1.2kg ratte potatoes
5g coarse Guérande sea salt
1 vanilla pod
20cl full fat milk
300g cold unsalted butter
Pinch of fine salt

———

A dash of olive oil
250g baby spinach leaves
1 clove of garlic
Pinch of fine salt

Line-caught whiting fried in butter and lemon, with braised artichokes and "pata negra" ham

PREPARATION TIME: 1 HOUR   COOKING TIME: 35 MINUTES   FOR 4 PEOPLE

• Scale, gut and fillet the whiting (or ask your fishmonger to do this for you). Rinse the fillets under cold running water and refrigerate.

Prepare all the artichokes by breaking the stems, removing the first layer of leaves and trimming the tips of the other leaves. Put them aside in a salad bowl with olive oil and lemon juice to prevent them going brown. Put the globe artichokes in a large saucepan, season with salt and pour in the white wine. Reduce by three quarters, then moisten with chicken stock, adding the basil leaves for seasoning. Cook for 30 minutes, or until the artichokes are tender. Once cooked, drain and put in the bowl of a Thermomix® or through a vegetable mouli. Keep the cooking liquid to one side. Mix a little of it with the purée as well as the cubes of cold butter. Season with salt if necessary. Put the purée to one side.

• Put the purple artichokes and the mushrooms in a saucepan. Season with salt and pour over the white wine. Reduce by three quarters, then moisten with the cooking liquid from the globe artichokes. Cook until the vegetables are nice and tender. Leave them in the cooking liquid.

• Heat a frying pan and add a dash of olive oil and the butter. Let it brown slightly and then add the whiting fillets, skin-side down, seasoned with salt. Cook both sides, basting with butter as they cook. When cooked, drain the fillets and place them on kitchen paper, skin-side up. Sprinkle with fleur de sel.

• Place the whiting fillets on dinner plates. Cut the purple artichokes in half and arrange them beside the fillets, as well as the halved onions and the mushrooms reheated in the artichoke cooking liquid. Decorate each plate with a few basil leaves and a slice of ham cut in half. Add a spoonful of hot veal jus. Serve the piping hot artichoke purée in an individual casserole dish.

2 line-caught whiting (500-600g each)
A dash of olive oil
15g slightly salted butter
Pinch of fine salt
Pinch of fleur de sel

—

8 purple artichokes
4 large globe artichokes
A dash of olive oil
Juice of 1 lemon
Pinch of fine salt
25g white wine
1 litre chicken stock
½ a bunch of basil
55g cold unsalted butter

—

24 mushrooms
Pinch of fine salt
25g white wine
25cl of the globe artichoke cooking liquid

—

4 small green onions, cooked in boiling salted water
1 small bunch of basil
4 thin slices of "pata negra" ham
10cl veal jus

Duck breast with cherries, ratte potato purée with Cassia cinnamon

PREPARATION TIME: 30 MINUTES   COOKING TIME: 1 HOUR   FOR 4 PEOPLE

• Remove the nerve and lightly trim the duck breasts. Keep the trimmings to one side to make the duck stock. Lightly score the fat in a chequered pattern, using a sharp knife. Keep the duck breasts in a cool place.

• Pour a few drops of groundnut oil into a saucepan and add the trimmings and the duck necks. Brown and add the butter. Leave them to caramelize. Then drain the fat. Keep the fat to baste the duck breast at the end of the cooking time. Add the peeled and chopped onion. Stir and add the veal stock. Cook for 35 to 45 minutes. Strain through a fine sieve, pressing down on the meat to extract all the juice. If the juice is reasonably thick, leave it in a bain-marie to keep warm. If not, reduce to a good consistency.

• Peel and rinse the potatoes. Drop them into a saucepan of cold, salted water and cook for 40 minutes. Heat the milk and a quarter of the butter in a second saucepan. When the potatoes are cooked, put them through a vegetable mill over the pan of milk. Stir thoroughly. Gradually add the rest of the cubed butter. Once the purée is nice and smooth, season with salt and the ground Cassia cinnamon.

• Wash the cherries, remove their stalks and then cut them in half to remove the stones. Set aside on a clean cloth.

• Heat a frying pan over a high heat, add the duck breasts, seasoned with salt on the fatty side, and brown them nicely. Turn them over, lower the heat and leave to cook for 3 to 5 minutes, or a little more depending on their size. Remove the duck breasts to a chopping board for five minutes. Drain the duck fat from the frying pan and throw in the cherries. Sauté them over a low heat for a few minutes until warm.

• Slice the duck breasts finely lengthways, then baste with the duck fat that you set aside earlier. Arrange the duck breasts on each serving plate. Decorate with a few cherries and add a few drops of the duck jus. Serve the cinnamon potato purée on the side.

4 small or 2 large duck breasts
(180-200g each)
A dash of groundnut oil
150g minced duck necks
15g slightly salted butter
½ sweet onion
75cl veal stock
Fine salt

———

1kg Ratte potatoes (from le Touquet)
5g coarse Guérande sea salt
20cl full fat milk
300g cold unsalted butter
Pinch of fine salt
1 stick of Cassia cinnamon
(Chinese cinnamon)

———

300g cherries (from Carpentras)

Tendron of veal en confit with smoked paprika and tagliatelle in citrus butter

PREPARATION TIME: 30 MINUTES   COOKING TIME: 2 HOURS 30   FOR 4 PEOPLE

• Preheat the oven to 140°C (280°F, gas mark 4-5). Peel the onions and chop them finely, then put to one side. Dry the veal tendrons on kitchen paper. Put a frying pan or sauté pan on a high heat and add a dash of groundnut oil. Season the tendrons with fine salt and smoked paprika. Add to the pan and brown them on both sides. Lower the heat and add the butter, then leave the tendrons to caramelize. Add the chopped onions, the crushed garlic and the sprig of thyme. Cover and leave to cook gently for 15 minutes. Deglaze with white wine. Leave to reduce by half then add the veal stock. Bring to the boil, then cover and put in the oven to cook for two hours.

• Mix the butter with the lime zest and juice in a large bowl. Put aside.

• Take the veal chops from the oven and put them back on a medium heat. Use a spoon to baste them regularly until the cooking juices have reduced and the meat is nicely glazed.

• Drop the fresh tagliatelle into a large saucepan of boiling salted water and leave to cook for four minutes. When cooked, drain in a colander and rinse under cold water. Put a good knob of the citrus butter in a hot frying or sauté pan and add the tagliatelle. Coat well in butter. Check the seasoning for salt.

• Roll the tagliatelle around a fork and place a pile on a large plate. Place the glazed veal next to it. Serve immediately.

2 white onions
4 tendrons of veal (200g each)
A dash of groundnut oil
Pinch of fine salt
A good pinch of smoked paprika
15g slightly salted butter
1 clove of garlic
1 sprig of thyme
20cl white wine
25cl veal stock

———

30g unsalted butter
Juice and zest of 1 lime

———

5g coarse Guérande sea salt
600g fresh tagliatelle
Pinch of table salt

Fricassée of calf's sweetbreads, petit pois cooked with Ibaïona bacon, creamy morel sauce

PREPARATION TIME: 1 HOUR   COOKING TIME: 40 MINUTES   FOR 4 PEOPLE

• Drop the sweetbreads into a large pan of boiling water, salted with the coarse sea salt, and cook for 10 minutes. Drain and refresh in a large bowl of iced water. Drain again and peel them. Put them aside in a cool place.

• Place the dried morels in a bowl of water. Leave them to soak for 10 to 15 minutes, then drain them and keep the soaking water. Pass it through a fine sieve. Pour a dash of olive oil into a saucepan, add the morels and season. Cook the morels until their juices run. Pour in the Banjuls wine and leave to reduce by half. Add the veal stock and cook for a few minutes. Pour in the soaking water and reduce by three quarters. Add the cream and bring to the boil, then lower the heat and leave to cook for 20 minutes. Stir the cream and pass it through a fine sieve. Keep it warm in a bain-marie.

• Wash the fresh morels in a bowl of warm water. Do this three times to get them clean and then drain. Pour a dash of olive oil in a frying pan and add the morels. Season and cook for three minutes. Drain on kitchen paper. Blanch the peas in boiling, salted water. Remove a quarter of the peas, refresh them in a bowl of iced water and drain on a piece of kitchen paper in a cold place. Continue cooking the remaining peas. Then drain, refresh in iced water and put in the bowl of a mixer or Thermomix®. Add a ladleful of hot chicken stock and the cubes of cold butter. Check the seasoning for salt. Cook the onions in the same way, refresh in iced water and drain.

• Cut the bacon into small cubes (0.5cm pieces). Brown them quickly on the griddle. Leave on a piece of kitchen paper. Pour a dash of groundnut oil into a hot frying pan, then add the seasoned and floured sweetbreads. Leave them to brown. Add the butter and brown. Pour in the veal stock, the whole peas and the diced bacon, and cook for a few minutes.

• Place a spoonful of the pea purée in each cocotte, then the sweetbread, ham and pea mixture on top. Add the morels and onions. Whisk the morel sauce until frothy using a hand blender and pour over the top.

400g calf's sweetbreads
5g coarse Guérande sea salt

———

100g dried morels
A dash of olive oil
Pinch of fine salt
A twist of freshly milled pepper
5cl Banyuls (a dessert wine from the Pyrenées)
5cl veal stock
50cl double cream

———

100g fresh morels
A dash of olive oil
Pinch of table salt
A twist of freshly milled pepper
250g petit pois
5g coarse Guérande sea salt
10cl chicken stock
25g cold unsalted butter
4 salad onions

———

200g Ibaïona bacon
A dash of groundnut oil
Pinch of fine salt
A twist of freshly milled pepper
25g wheat flour
10g slightly salted butter
5cl veal stock

Shoulder of lamb confit, with ras-el-hanout and quinoa tabbouleh

COOKING AND PREPARATION TIME THE DAY BEFORE: 7 HOURS
PREPARATION TIME: 1 HOUR   FOR 4 PEOPLE

• The night before, preheat the oven to 140°C (280°F, gas mark 4-5). Put a frying pan over a high heat with the olive oil, peeled garlic and thyme. Season the shoulder of lamb with ras-el-hanout and fine salt and tie it neatly. Brown it evenly on all sides in the frying pan. Once it is well browned, leave it on a plate with the garlic and thyme to cool, then move it on to an ovenproof dish. Pour over the lamb stock and put in the oven to cook for four hours, basting regularly. Check the cooking of the lamb with the blade of a knife. Pierce the shoulder: if the juices still run and the flesh is firm, cook for a little longer. Then allow the meat to rest in its cooking juices for two hours.

• The next day, bring a saucepan of water to the boil. Put in the quinoa and cook it according to the packet instructions. Then rinse it in cold water to refresh it. Rinse the pepper, remove the seeds and then dice it finely. Rinse and peel the preserved lemon, keeping only the peel. Dice it finely. Soak the currants in twice their volume of boiling water.

• Remove the shoulder of lamb from its cooking juices. Strain the jus through a fine sieve and, if necessary, reduce it to obtain a smooth, thick sauce. Cut the lamb into nice 2cm thick slices. Lay them flat in a sauté pan and cover with the reduced cooking juices. Simmer until the juice glazes the slices of lamb. Reheat the quinoa with the olive oil, add the peppers, lemon and currants and then arrange everything on the plates. Finish with a sprinkling of chopped coriander.

A dash of olive oil
2 cloves of garlic
1 sprig of thyme
1 boned and rolled shoulder
of lamb (1.5kg)
6g ras-el-hanout
6g fine salt
50cl lamb stock

300g quinoa
30g pimiento del piquillo
(small red pepper)
1 preserved lemon (in brine)
30g dried currants
A dash of olive oil
½ a bunch of coriander

Beef chuck pot-au-feu, pan-fried foie gras with autumn vegetables

PREPARATION THE DAY BEFORE: 5 HOURS + 1 RESTING OVERNIGHT

PREPARATION TIME: 30 MINUTES   COOKING TIME: 30 MINUTES   FOR 4 PEOPLE

• The night before, peel the vegetables in the bouquet garni and chop into small (1cm) cubes. Remove any nerves from the beef, then put it to cook in a saucepan of cold water with the coarse sea salt. Bring to the boil. Skim the surface with a slotted spoon, then add the bouquet garni, thyme, bay leaf and clove. Simmer for five hours. When cooked, drain the meat and roll it up tightly in cling film. Put the roll in the fridge and leave overnight. Sieve the stock, without pressing down on it, into a large bowl, cover with cling film and leave in the fridge overnight.

• The next day, remove the fat from the stock with a slotted spoon. Keep just the clear stock, leaving the dregs in the bottom of the bowl. Peel and wash all the carrots, then cut them into small wedges (about 1cm thick). Cut off the stalks of the mini turnips and remove the top leaves from the mini leeks. Trim the leeks to 8cm. Pour half of the clear stock into a saucepan and bring to the boil. Drop in the vegetables and cook until nice and tender.

• Heat the blade of a sharp knife in hot water. Cut a criss-cross pattern on one side of each foie gras fillet with this knife. Season with fine salt and freshly milled pepper. Cut the beef into 2cm thick slices and reheat it in the stock with the vegetables. Brown the fillets of foie gras on both sides in a hot frying pan, then place them on kitchen paper. Sprinkle with the fleur de sel de Guérande.

• Arrange the vegetables in the cocottes. Sprinkle with chopped chives. Place the slices of beef on top, and then the fillets of foie gras. Finish by adding the piping hot clear stock. Season the meat with fleur de sel and a twist of freshly milled pepper. Decorate with sprigs of chervil.

One bouquet garni (1 carrot,
1 onion, 1 stick of celery)
1.5kg of beef chuck steak
10g coarse Guérande sea salt
1 sprig of thyme
1 bay leaf
1 clove
_____
2 carrots
2 yellow carrots
8 mini-turnips
8 mini-leeks
_____
4 fresh fillets of foie gras (60g each)
Pinch of fine salt
A twist of freshly milled pepper
Fleur de sel de Guérande
_____
½ bunch of chives, chopped
Pinch of fleur de sel de Guérande
A twist of freshly milled pepper
8 sprigs of chervil

Sirloin steak with a shallot confit, beef jus and home-made chips

PREPARATION THE DAY BEFORE: 45 MINUTES + 1 RESTING OVERNIGHT

PREPARATION TIME: 30 MINUTES   COOKING TIME: 20 MINUTES   FOR 4 PEOPLE

• The night before, cut the stewing steak into cubes. Pour a dash of groundnut oil into a saucepan on a high heat. Throw in the beef cubes and brown them on all sides. Add the onion and let it brown. Next add the butter and let the ingredients caramelize. Remove any excess fat and deglaze with the sherry vinegar. Add the peppercorns. Leave to reduce by three quarters before adding the veal stock. Bring to the boil, cover and cook for 45 minutes. When cooked, strain the juices into a large bowl, pressing down on the meat. Leave in the fridge for 8 hours or overnight.

• The next day, remove the bowl from the fridge. Use a spoon to remove any fat that has formed on the surface of the stock. Pour the stock into a saucepan and let it reduce to a syrupy consistency. Put aside.

• Peel and finely chop the shallots, then rinse them under cold water in a small colander. Put the shallots into a saucepan, pour in the red wine and add the sprig of thyme, bay leaf and the crushed garlic. Cook over a low heat until the shallots have absorbed all of the wine. Put aside.

• Peel the potatoes and cut into chips. Rinse in cold water and keep them in a bowl of clean water. Heat the oil in a deep fryer programmed for 140°C (280°F). Drop the chips in for 4-6 minutes, then drain them. Raise the temperature of the oil to 180°C (350°F).

• Take the steaks from the fridge 15 minutes before cooking to bring them up to room temperature. Heat the groundnut oil in a frying pan and add the butter. Let it foam and when it turns golden add the steak, seasoned beforehand with fine salt and freshly milled pepper. Cook the steaks on a high heat for two minutes on each side.

• Gently reheat the shallots in a small saucepan. To finish cooking the chips, drop them into the 180°C (350°F) oil for three minutes. Dry them well and season with fine salt. Place them in individual serving dishes.

• Slice the steaks and place them on hot serving plates. Cover them carefully with the shallot confit and the beef jus. Sprinkle with fleur de sel and add a twist of freshly milled pepper. Decorate with sprigs of chervil.

150g stewing steak
A dash of groundnut oil
1 onion
15g slightly salted butter
5cl sherry vinegar
10 black peppercorns
75cl veal stock

———

4 grey shallots
50cl red wine
A sprig of thyme
1 bay leaf
1 clove of garlic

———

1kg potatoes suitable for frying
2 litres cooking oil
Pinch of fine salt

———

4 sirloin steaks (140-150g each)
A dash of groundnut oil
15g slightly salted butter
Pinch of fine salt
A twist of freshly milled pepper

———

Pinch fleur de sel Guérande
A twist of freshly milled pepper
½ a bunch of chervil

Braised beef cheek with mild spices, macaroni gratin with mature Parmesan cheese

PREPARATION TIME: 1 HOUR   COOKING TIME: 4 HOURS 30   FOR 4 PEOPLE

• Remove any nerves from the beef (or ask your butcher to do this) and wrap it in a clean cloth. Keep it in the fridge. Peel and wash the vegetables for the bouquet garni, then dice them into 1cm cubes. Pour the red wine into a saucepan and bring to the boil. Burn off the alcohol and reduce the heat. When the flame goes out, add the mixed spices. Put aside. Pour the groundnut oil into a casserole dish and put on a high heat. Season the beef, then brown it on all sides in the oil. Remove from the casserole when golden. Add the butter to the casserole dish, now over a low heat, and allow it to foam. Add the diced vegetables.

• Once the vegetables begin to sweat and colour, remove them to a plate. Remove the oil from the casserole, turn up the heat and deglaze with the spiced red wine. Scrape the juices from the bottom of the casserole with a spatula. Let the wine reduce by three quarters. Put the meat and the vegetables back into the casserole and cover with the rest of the wine so that the beef is well covered. Bring gently to the boil, then cover and put in a fan-heated oven for four hours at 200°C (390°F, gas mark 6-7). Turn the meat regularly.

• Once cooked, remove the beef with a slotted spoon and put it into a dish. Shred it and check for seasoning. Strain the jus through a fine strainer and reduce it slowly in the casserole dish until you have a smooth sauce.

• Drop the macaroni into a saucepan of salted, boiling water and cook for eight minutes. Drain and leave to cool on a baking sheet. Cover with cling film. When the macaroni is cold, cut it into 1cm thick rounds. Put the cream in a saucepan and bring to the boil, then add the Parmesan, whisking all the time. Bring it back to the boil, then pour into a jug or bowl and put aside.

• Turn the oven to grill. Reheat the shredded beef and the cooking juices in a casserole dish. Divide it out among four individual cast-iron casserole dishes. Cover with the reduced cooking juices. Roll the macaroni in the Parmesan cream and cover the meat with them. Sprinkle with grated Parmesan cheese. Put under the grill for eight minutes until golden on top. Serve hot with sprigs of chervil and a side salad dressed with a vinaigrette of white balsamic vinegar and olive oil.

1kg beef cheek
1 bouquet garni (1 carrot, 1 onion, 1 stick of celery)
1 litre full-bodied red wine
Mixed spices (Chinese cinnamon, star anise, peppercorns, clove)
A dash of groundnut oil
Pinch of fine salt
A twist of freshly milled pepper
25g unsalted butter

500g macaroni
5g coarse Guérande sea salt
300g single cream
150g mature Parmesan, grated

50g mature Parmesan, grated
½ a bunch of chervil
250g baby salad leaves
A dash of white balsamic vinegar
A dash of olive oil
Pinch of fine salt

Pork chops with a satay sauce, dauphine potatoes

PREPARATION TIME: 1 HOUR   COOKING TIME: 1 HOUR   FOR 4 PEOPLE

• Put the water, butter and 15g fine salt in a saucepan and bring to the boil, then lower the heat immediately. Remove from the heat and add the flour, beating all the time with a spatula. Add enough flour to absorb all the liquid so the mixture no longer sticks to your fingers. Once all the moisture has evaporated, pour the mixture into a large bowl. Beat the eggs together then, using the spatula, gradually incorporate the beaten eggs into the mixture. When the eggs are fully incorporated and the mixture is smooth, add the mashed potato and mix again. Season with the grated nutmeg. Make small 25g balls and refrigerate.

• Remove the rind from the pork chops and clean the bones by scraping them with a small knife. Put each one in an airtight bag. Programme the thermoplongeur (machine for cooking sous vide) to 64°C (150°F). Put the chops in for one hour. When cooked, drain and drop into a basin of iced water. After 15 minutes, drain again and put in a cool place. Reprogramme the thermoplongeur to 52.2°C (130°F). Just before serving, put the cooked chops back in the thermoplongeur for 15 minutes.

• Heat the oil in a deep fryer to 160°C (320°F). Drop in the dauphine potatoes and leave to cook until they turn golden. Drain and place on a dish covered with kitchen paper. Season with fine salt. Keep warm.

• Melt the butter in a frying pan and add the satay powder. Stir over a low heat. Take the pork chops from their airtight packages and dry them. Place them on a griddle and brown on each side, then put them in the pan with the butter and satay. Baste with the butter.

• Place the chops on serving plates. Decorate with thyme. Arrange the Dauphine potatoes on the side or serve in individual casserole dishes.

50cl water
80g unsalted butter
250g flour
6 eggs
1kg boiled potatoes, mashed
Pinch of grated nutmeg
Cooking oil
Fine salt

___

4 farmhouse pork chops, bone in (500g each)
150g unsalted butter
75g satay powder
4 small sprigs of thyme

The Chardenoux des Prés pure Aubrac beefburger, with potato waffles

PREPARATION TIME: 1 HOUR   COOKING TIME: 1 HOUR   FOR 4 PEOPLE

• Peel the potatoes and slice them thinly using a serrated mandolin. Give the potato a quarter turn each time you pass it over the mandolin to get the criss-cross effect. Put the waffles in a large bowl of water as you cut them to avoid them going brown. Heat the oil in the deep fryer to 140°C (280°F). Prepare a cooking tray with kitchen paper and a slotted spoon. Drop the potato waffles into the deep fryer for five minutes then drain them. Raise the temperature of the oil to 170°C (340°F). Just before serving, drop the waffles in again and leave until they turn golden. When cooked, drain them on kitchen paper and season with fine salt.

• In a large bowl, mix the egg yolk with the Dijon mustard. Season with salt and mix well, then trickle in the grape seed oil, stirring all the time. The consistency of the mayonnaise should be fairly thick. Add the ketchup, Worcestershire sauce and Tabasco® sauce and mix again. Add the lemon juice and cognac to finish. The sauce should be nice and thick. Check the seasoning for salt. Keep cool.

• Preheat the grill. Cut the buns in half widthways. Put the top halves under the grill to brown. Put aside. Spread a large spoonful of sauce on the bottom halves and arrange the little gem lettuce leaves and 2 slices of tomato on each one.

• Season the burgers. Pour a dash of groundnut oil on a griddle, then add the burgers and cook according to your taste. Remove from the griddle just before they finish cooking, sprinkle over the cheddar and put them under the grill for a few moments to melt the cheese. When cooked, remove the burgers from the grill and place them on top of the tomatoes. Grill the bacon on the griddle. Brown both sides then place on top of the burgers. Break the quail eggs directly onto the griddle, fry them, then lay them on top of the bacon. Sprinkle with fleur de sel. Put the toasted bun tops back onto the burgers. Serve with extra sauce in a ramekin and the potato waffles in a bowl.

---

5 large potatoes
Cooking oil
Pinch of fine salt

---

1 egg yolk
5g Dijon mustard
Pinch of fine salt
25cl grape seed oil
10g ketchup
1 teaspoon Worcestershire sauce
6 drops of Tabasco® sauce
The juice of ½ a lemon
1 teaspoon cognac

---

4 sesame buns
12 leaves of little gem lettuce
8 slices of vine tomato
4 Aubrac beef burgers (Aubrac is a French breed of cattle raised for beef)
Pinch of table salt
A twist of freshly milled pepper
A dash of groundnut oil
80g mature cheddar cheese, grated
4 slices of smoked streaky bacon
4 quails eggs
Fleur de sel de Guérande

Bresse chicken thighs braised in Sancerre wine, green asparagus with Ibaïona bacon

PREPARATION TIME: 1 HOUR   COOKING TIME: 40 MINUTES   FOR 4 PEOPLE

• Heat a dash of groundnut oil in a saucepan and add the chicken thighs. Fry until brown on all sides. Add the butter and continue cooking until caramelized. Peel and dice the onion and add this along with the thyme and garlic (unpeeled). Cook for another 10 minutes. Remove the saucepan from the heat and remove any excess fat. Put back on a high heat and pour in the veal stock. Bring to the boil, then lower the heat and cook for 30 minutes, until the liquid is concentrated and slightly thickened. Strain the jus and keep warm in a bain-marie.

• Bone the four chicken thighs. Season them and tie them neatly. Roll each one tightly in cling film. Pour the Sancerre wine and the stock into a saucepan. Bring to the boil then drop in the chicken rolls, cover and turn off the heat. Leave to cook for 35 minutes. When cooked, drain the rolls and put them to one side exactly as they are. Next, reduce the cooking jus by three quarters. Add the cream and reduce again by half. Add the lemon juice. Use a hand blender to finish the sauce with the cubes of butter. Season. Put the sauce to one side.

• Remove the small leaves from the asparagus stems and trim them to 12cm in length. Bring a large saucepan of salted water to the boil. Drop in the asparagus and let them cook until nice and tender. Drain them and drop into a basin of iced water. Drain them quickly again. Cut off the tips at 4cm, chop the rest of the stem into 2cm rounds. Put aside in a cool place.

• Remove the cling film from the chicken rolls and dry them. Pour a dash of groundnut oil into a hot frying pan and add the slightly salted butter. As soon as it is golden, add the chicken rolls and brown for a few minutes until crispy and hot. Baste them with the foaming butter. Untie the chicken and slice each roll into five pieces.

• Pour the chicken stock into a sauté pan. Bring to the boil and add the butter. Add the tips and the rounds of the asparagus, glaze them for five minutes. Add the diced bacon to the smoking hot pan to brown. Drain on kitchen paper.

• Use a hand blender to give the sauce a frothy consistency. Coat the chicken with the hot stock. Arrange the asparagus pieces and the diced bacon in a cocotte. Add the chicken pieces and coat with the emulsified sauce. Decorate with asparagus tips.

2 Bresse chicken thighs
A dash of groundnut oil
15g slightly salted butter
1 onion
1 sprig of thyme
1 clove of garlic
2 litres veal stock
5cl chicken stock

---

4 Bresse chicken thighs
Pinch of fine salt
A twist of freshly milled pepper
50cl white Sancerre wine
50cl chicken stock
50cl double cream
The juice of ½ a lemon
15g cold unsalted butter
Fine salt and freshly ground pepper

---

12 medium grade green asparagus
5g coarse Guérande sea salt
5cl chicken stock
10g slightly salted butter
200g Ibaïona bacon chopped into 0.5 cm cubes

A dash of groundnut oil
10g slightly salted butter

Desserts

Queen Victoria pineapple, lime and fromage blanc sorbet

PREPARATION TIME: 30 MINUTES (+ TIME IN THE ICE-CREAM MAKER)
COOKING TIME: 10 MINUTES   FOR 4 PEOPLE

• Remove the top and bottom of the pineapples, then remove the skin using a serrated knife by following the natural shape of the pineapple and avoiding cutting into the flesh. Use a vegetable peeler to remove the eyes from the flesh.

• Cut four slices of pineapple per person, in other words, eight slices from each pineapple. Use a small cutter (1cm in diameter) to remove the hard core in the centre of each slice. Immerse the pineapple rings in the syrup and put aside in a cool place.

• Put the water and sugar in a saucepan and stir. Bring to the boil before adding the lemon juice, then stir again. Put the fromage blanc in a bowl and pour the syrup over the top. Add the lime zest, grated with a Microplane® grater. Transfer the mixture to the freezer bowl of an ice-cream maker and start the programme. Once finished, keep the sorbet in the freezer.

• Arrange four slices of pineapple in a stack, slightly overlapping, in each presentation dish. Pour over a spoonful of syrup. Place a spoonful of sorbet on top. Finish by sprinkling over a little grated lime zest.

2 Queen Victoria pineapples
15cl light sugar syrup

———

350g water
150g caster sugar
50g lemon juice
250g fromage blanc (or fromage frais, can be substituted with Greek yoghurt)
The zest of 1 unwaxed lime

———

The zest of ½ unwaxed lime for decoration

Dark chocolate soufflé

PREPARATION TIME: 15 MINUTES   COOKING TIME: 10 MINUTES   FOR 4 PEOPLE

• Grease four individual soufflé dishes thoroughly with the softened butter using a pastry brush. Sprinkle the dishes with sugar, then turn them to make sure the sides are well covered with sugar. Turn upside down to tap out any excess sugar.

• Break the chocolate into pieces and put it with the butter in a bain-marie (a bowl sitting over a saucepan of simmering water). When the chocolate has melted, stir it carefully. Remove from the bain-marie, transfer to a large bowl and leave to cool. Preheat the oven to 180°C (350°F, gas mark 6).

• Break the egg whites into the bowl of an electric mixer and whisk them up using the wire whisk attachment. As soon as they begin to form peaks, add the sugar gradually. Once nearly stiff, add the egg yolks and mix again for a few seconds.

• Add a quarter of the whisked egg whites to the large bowl with the chocolate and fold in carefully using a spatula. Then gently fold in the rest of the whisked egg whites. Put the mixture in a piping bag with a large round nozzle.

• Divide the soufflé mixture between the soufflé dishes, filling each one generously. Smooth the surface of each with a large spatula. Clean the sides of the dishes, then separate the soufflé mixture slightly from the edges of the dishes by running your thumb and index finger around the inside edges.

• Place the soufflés on a baking tray and put in the oven for 8-10 minutes. Do not open the door of the oven. Once cooked, take them out of the oven, sprinkle with icing sugar and serve immediately.

25g soft unsalted butter
to grease the soufflé dishes
25g caster sugar for
the soufflé dishes

250g grand cru (finest quality)
dark chocolate, 64% cocoa solids
50g unsalted butter
8 egg whites
80g caster sugar
3 egg yolks

Icing sugar to decorate

Bourbon vanilla cream pots, raspberries with wild anise

PREPARATION TIME: 3 HOURS 15   COOKING TIME: 20 MINUTES   FOR 4 PEOPLE

• Soak the sheets of gelatine in cold water for two hours before using them. Split the vanilla pods in half lengthways and scrape the insides with the point of a knife to extract the seeds. Heat the cream in a saucepan. Pour the hot cream into a bowl and mix in the vanilla seeds and sugar. Drain and squeeze out the sheets of gelatine with your hands and add them to the cream mixture. Mix again and pour the mixture into four small pots. Leave in the fridge for three hours until the cream has set.

• Carefully mix the raspberries, caster sugar and water together in a sauté pan. Heat gently, crushing the raspberries, and leave to cook over a low heat for 10 minutes. Reduce the raspberry juice in this way until it is darker and thicker. When cooked, pass this coulis through a fine sieve to make it nice and smooth. Keep cool until ready to serve.

• Pour the cold raspberry coulis onto the vanilla creams. Place three raspberries, with the hole facing upwards, in each pot of vanilla cream, then fill them with raspberry coulis. Sprinkle over a few seeds of wild anise and serve.

2 sheets of gelatine
2 Bourbon vanilla pods
450g double cream
30g caster sugar

———

150g raspberries
15g caster sugar
5cl mineral water

———

12 raspberries for decoration
A few grains of wild anise
for decoration

Pear and chocolate tart

PREPARATION TIME: 45 MINUTES   COOKING TIME: 30 MINUTES   FOR 4 PEOPLE

• Put the butter in the bowl of your mixer and beat until smooth and firm. Split the vanilla pod in half lengthways and scrape the inside with the point of a knife to extract the flesh. Mix the ground almonds, cornmeal, fine salt, icing sugar and vanilla flesh together in a mixing bowl. Pour this mixture into the butter and mix together, then add the beaten egg and flour in three parts, mixing all the time. When it forms a ball of dough, put in the fridge for 20 minutes.

• Put the icing sugar, ground almonds and custard powder into the bowl of a mixer and stir together. Fit the flat blade to the mixer, add the softened butter to the bowl and mix. Beat the eggs and add them slowly, mixing all the time. Pour in the rum and transfer the cream to a large bowl. Keep in the fridge. Once the cream is properly chilled, add the chocolate pearls.

• Take the dough from the fridge and roll out to a thickness of 3-4mm using a rolling pin. Place the dough in a plain tart ring for four people. Put in the fridge for 20 minutes. Heat the oven to 180°C (350°F, gas mark 6). Once the dough has chilled, bake for 10 minutes. Remove from the oven and pour the almond cream into the tart ring. Cut the pears into cubes and place these on top. Bake for another 20 minutes.

• When you take it out of the oven, sprinkle the tart with icing sugar and decorate with a few chocolate pearls.

95g unsalted butter
1 vanilla pod
28g ground almonds
52g cornmeal
1g fine salt
89.5g icing sugar
1 egg
182g flour

117g icing sugar
147g ground almonds
14g custard powder
117g softened butter
1½ eggs
14g rum
100g chocolate pearls

2 pears in syrup
Icing sugar
25g chocolate pearls

Lemon shortbread, organic wild strawberries from Andalusia

PREPARATION THE DAY BEFORE: 40 MINUTES + 24 HOURS RESTING TIME

PREPARATION TIME: 45 MINUTES   COOKING TIME: 15 MINUTES   FOR 4 PEOPLE

• The night before, leave the sheets of gelatine in a large bowl of cold water. Let them soak for at least 20 minutes. Pour the lime purée into a large bowl and mix in 30g sugar. Put the egg whites into the bowl of a mixer and whisk them up with the remaining 30g sugar. Pour a quarter of the lime mixture into a small saucepan, heat and stir in the well-drained gelatine. Add the remainder of the lime mixture and stir again. Pour all of the lime mixture into the egg whites and mix carefully. Slowly add the whipped cream and then pour the mixture into 6cm diameter hemisphere moulds. Chill for 8 hours.

• Sift the flour and the baking powder into a large bowl using a fine sieve. Beat the sugar, salt and egg yolks together in the mixer bowl using the whisk accessory. Mix until it becomes pale yellow and fluffy. Replace the whisk accessory with the flat blade. Incorporate the softened butter a little at a time, then add the sifted flour and baking powder. Once the dough is nice and smooth, put it to rest in the fridge for 24 hours.

• The next day, preheat the oven to 180°C (350°F, gas mark 6). Roll out the dough to a thickness of ½cm on a baking tray covered with greaseproof paper. Bake in the oven for 12 minutes. Once cooked, remove the tray from the oven. Cut out four circles from the pastry using a 6cm round cutter. Leave to cool at room temperature.

• Melt the white chocolate with the cocoa butter and pour into a chocolate spray gun. Spray the lime cream hemispheres with the chocolate and leave them to chill in the fridge. This step can only be carried out by patisserie professionals.

• Top and tail the gariguette strawberries, cut them in half and put them in a small saucepan with the sugar. Cook over a low heat for 15 minutes. When cooked, put them in the blender and then pass through a fine sieve. Put to one side.

• Put a shortbread circle in the centre of each plate. Place a lime cream hemisphere on top. Cut the wild strawberries in half and decorate right the way around the edge. Finish with a few drops of the strawberry coulis and decorate with verbena leaves.

9½ sheets of gelatine
130g lime purée
60g caster sugar
2 egg whites
230g whipped double cream

175g flour
11g baking powder
125g caster sugar
1g fine salt
3 egg yolks
125g softened unsalted butter

250g Valhrona® white chocolate
250g cocoa butter

15g caster sugar
125g Gariguette strawberries

125g organic wild strawberries from Andalusia
A bunch of fresh verbena

Pancakes with Gariguette strawberries, passion fruit sorbet

PREPARATION TIME: 1 HOUR (+ TIME IN THE ICE-CREAM MAKER)
COOKING TIME: 20 MINUTES   FOR 4 PEOPLE

• Put the flour, sugar and salt in a large bowl. Split the vanilla pod in two lengthways, then scrape out the inside with the point of a knife to take out the seeds. Add them to the flour mixture. Also add the eggs and milk, then pour in the melted butter. Mix again. Put the pancake batter in the fridge for 30 minutes.

• Open the passion fruits and sieve the flesh into a mixing bowl. Put the sugar and water into a small saucepan. Bring to the boil, then pour into the bowl with the passion fruit juice. Mix well and pour this mixture into the ice-cream maker. Start the machine. Once the sorbet is made, keep in the freezer.

• Top and tail the strawberries and cut them into four, then mix them carefully with the icing sugar in a large bowl.

• Use kitchen paper to spread a little oil around the pancake pan. Heat the pan and then pour in a ladleful of pancake mixture. Cook until the pancake turns golden, then flip it over and cook until the other side is golden too. Repeat to make eight pancakes. Then spread each pancake with a knob of melted butter. Fold into four and arrange two nicely on each plate.

• Place eight strawberry quarters on each pancake and add a spoonful of passion fruit sorbet. Decorate with a spoonful of the strawberry coulis.

250g flour
100g caster sugar
Pinch of fine salt
1 vanilla pod
4 eggs
75cl milk
120g unsalted butter

500g passion fruit juice (made from approx. 2½kg fruit)
75g water
75g caster sugar

250g Gariguette strawberries
20g caster sugar

5cl grape seed oil
25g unsalted butter
4 tablespoons strawberry coulis

Rice pudding with Bourbon vanilla, mango coulis

PREPARATION TIME: 15 MINUTES   COOKING TIME: 30 MINUTES   FOR 4 PEOPLE

• Pour the water, salt and rice in a saucepan. Cook the rice for 10 minutes, then add the milk, sugar and vanilla pods, which have been split in half lengthways and scraped out. Cook for about another 20 minutes over a very low heat. Once cooked, the rice should be nice and soft. Keep cool.

• Peel the mango and scrape out the flesh. Put it in the blender and then pass through a fine sieve to obtain a coulis. Keep this coulis in the fridge until ready to serve.

• Pour the rice pudding into a large bowl and carefully stir in the vanilla Chantilly cream. Divide this mixture into four ramekins. Decorate each with half a dried vanilla pod and a spoonful of mango coulis.

200g water
1g fine salt
125g Arborio risotto rice
50cl full fat milk
45g caster sugar
2 Bourbon vanilla pods
50g Chantilly cream with Bourbon vanilla

———

1 Avion mango
2 dried Bourbon vanilla pods

Pain perdu with cherries, Sicilian pistachio ice cream

PREPARATION TIME: 1 HOUR (+ TIME IN THE ICE-CREAM MAKER)
COOKING TIME: 20 MINUTES   FOR 4 PEOPLE

• Put the sugar and egg yolks in a large bowl and beat together with a whisk. Add the milk and hot cream, then mix again with a whisk. Transfer the mixture to a saucepan and cook over a very low heat for seven minutes. Whisk as it thickens to make a custard. Turn off the heat as soon as the custard starts to coat the whisk. Remove the pan from the heat and fold in the pistachio paste with a spatula. Mix well and leave to cool for a few minutes. Once the custard is cool, almost cold, cover with cling film and refrigerate. Turn on the ice cream maker and pour the pistachio custard into the freezer bowl. Leave in the ice cream maker until it has reached the consistency of a rich smooth ice cream. Put aside in the freezer.

• Split the vanilla pods in half lengthways and scrape out the inside with the point of a knife to extract the seeds. Mix the milk, sugar, eggs and vanilla seeds in a large bowl. Use a bread knife to cut the brioche neatly into 2cm thick slices. Soak each slice in the egg and milk mixture. Drain them immediately and place on a rack with a plate underneath.

• Heat a non-stick frying pan and melt the butter in it. Place the slices of brioche in the pan and fry them lightly. Sprinkle over the sugar. Continue frying until lightly golden on both sides. A caramel sauce will form in the pan - use this to baste the brioche as it cooks. Once coloured on both sides, remove the brioche from the pan and place on the rack.

• Wash all the cherries and remove the stones. Put 150g of them into a juice extractor, then strain the juice obtained through a muslin cloth. Pour into a saucepan and heat until it has reduced by half. The coulis should be nice and syrupy. Put aside in a small bowl at room temperature. Keep the rest of the cherries in the fridge. Remember to take them out about an hour before serving.

• Put the hot pain perdu on a flat plate and arrange the fresh cherries on top of it. Decorate the edge of the plate with a few drops of the cherry coulis. Add a nice spoonful of Sicilian pistachio ice cream. To create the perfect spoonful, plunge a dessert spoon into hot water first, then scrape the spoon through the ice cream from the back to the front of the bowl to make a nice oval scoop.

70g caster sugar
3 egg yolks
250g full fat milk
250g double cream
75g Sicilian pistachio paste

---

2 vanilla pods
250g full fat milk
35g caster sugar + a little extra for cooking
3 eggs
4 slices from a brioche loaf
25g unsalted butter

400g fresh cherries

Chocolate éclair

PREPARATION TIME: 20 MINUTES + 12 HOURS   COOKING TIME: 25 MINUTES   FOR 4 PEOPLE

• Pour the milk, cream, egg yolks and sugar into a saucepan. Heat gently to a temperature of 83°C (180°F). When cooked, add the sheet of gelatine, soaked beforehand and drained well. Mix. Put the two types of chocolate in a large bowl and pour over the contents of the saucepan. Stir thoroughly until the mixture is smooth and creamy. Cover with cling film, allowing the cling film to touch the top of the mixture, and rest in the fridge for 12 hours.

• Put the water, butter, sugar and salt in a saucepan. Bring to the boil. Add the powdered milk, then bring back to the boil. Remove from the heat and add the flour, then stir well and leave on a very low heat to cook the starch in the flour. Pour this mixture into a large bowl. Beat the eggs separately in a small bowl, then incorporate them in three parts into the previous mixture, pouring in gradually each time. Use a spatula to mix well. The consistency of the choux pastry should be smooth without sticking to your fingers. Transfer it to a piping bag fitted with a large round nozzle.

• Preheat the oven to 160°C (320°F, gas mark 5-6). Pipe the choux pastry onto a baking sheet covered with greaseproof paper. Pipe individual tubes, 2cm wide by 11cm long, and space them out in staggered rows. Brush each one with beaten egg to help it turn golden. Bake in the oven for three minutes. When cooked, remove from the oven and leave to cool.

• Make two small holes on the bottom of each éclair and fill them with the chocolate cream. Then ice the éclairs with the chocolate icing and keep in the fridge until ready to serve.

170g full fat milk
170g single cream
2 egg yolks
20g caster sugar
1 sheet of gelatine
21g Valrhona "coeur de Guanaja"
dark chocolate chips or discs
65g Valrhona "Caraibe" dark chocolate
chips or discs

———

182g water
72g unsalted butter
3g caster sugar
2.5g fine salt
13g powdered milk
88g type 55 flour
3 eggs

———

1 egg yolk
40g chocolate icing

Salted caramel macarons

PREPARATION THE DAY BEFORE: 20 MINUTES + 24 HOURS RESTING TIME
PREPARATION TIME: 20 MINUTES   COOKING TIME: 25 MINUTES   FOR 4 PEOPLE

• Pour the cream into a saucepan and heat. Put the sugar in another saucepan and heat until it turns a deep yellow, then lower the heat and pour the hot cream onto the caramel. Whisk over the heat, paying attention to the boiling temperature. Add the sheet of gelatine, which should be soaked and drained beforehand. Stir again. Put the white chocolate in a mixing bowl and pour the hot mixture over it. Do this in three stages, mixing well in between. Add the condensed milk and fleur de sel. Mix with a hand blender, then add the ground almonds which should be heated to 50°C (120°F) beforehand. Leave this cream mixture in the fridge for 24 hours without stirring it. The next day, transfer it to a piping bag with a small round nozzle and put the bag back in the fridge. Whisk the egg whites in the bowl of an electric mixer with the coffee extract. Add the sugar and whisk until they form firm peaks. Mix the ground almonds and the icing sugar together into a fine powder. Transfer the whisked egg whites to a large mixing bowl, then pour the almond-sugar mixture on top. Mix them together. Don't worry too much about the egg whites collapsing, it is more important that the mixture is smooth and creamy without any air bubbles. However, be careful not to over mix it or it will become too runny.

• Preheat the oven to 150°C (300°F, gas mark 5). Put the macaron mixture into a piping bag fitted with a plain round medium sized nozzle (N° 8). Pipe small domes of the mixture (about 1½ cm in diameter) onto a baking sheet covered with greaseproof paper. Place them in staggered rows and space well apart (2cm between each one). Tap the baking sheet on the work surface to make sure the macarons all settle to a similar size. Place the baking sheet in a warm oven or near a current of air, so that a slight crust forms on the macarons. Once they no longer stick to your fingers, bake in the oven for 12 minutes. They should be shiny and uniform in colour. Try picking off a couple of the macarons. If they don't come away easily, they need a few more minutes cooking time.

• When cooked, take them out of the oven, set aside to cool and then take them off the paper. Put them on a baking sheet in pairs of matching size. Garnish half the macaron shells with the caramel and close them with the other shells. Keep in the fridge.

Tip: you may prefer to prepare the macarons two days before assembly.

200g double cream
67.5g caster sugar
1 sheet of gelatine
150g white chocolate
20g condensed milk
1g fleur de sel de Guérande
12.5g ground almonds

―――――――

3 egg whites
4 drops of Trablit® coffee extract
100g caster sugar
100g ground almonds
100g icing sugar

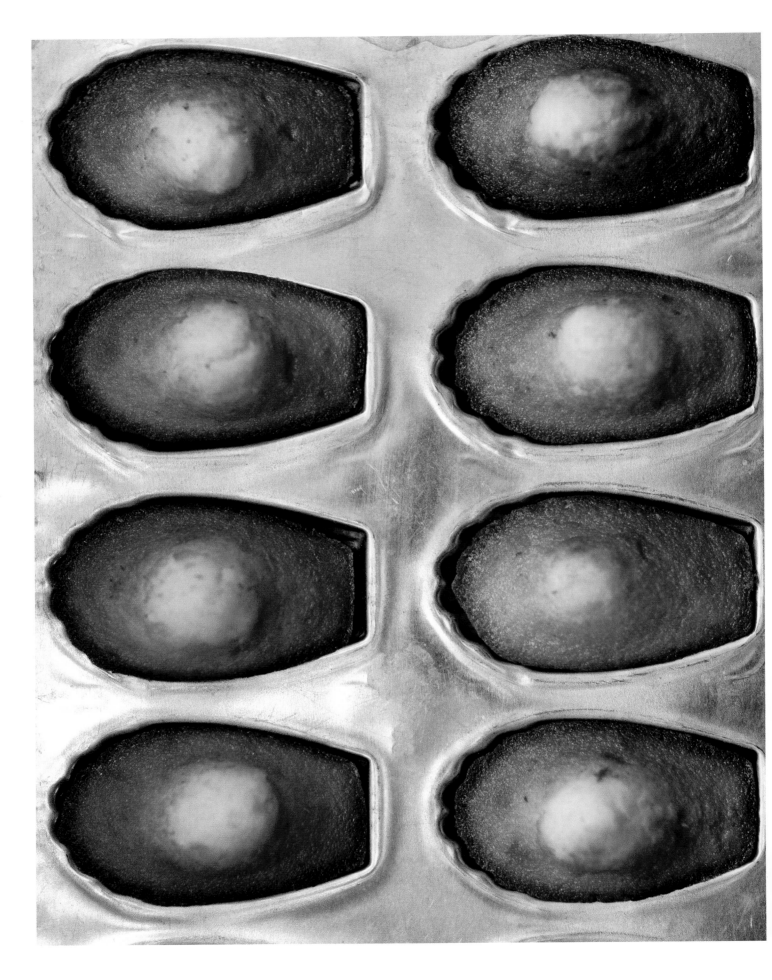

Table of Recipes

Index

Acknowledgements

"I wanted to write this book in order to share with my clients the passion I felt
for this traditional bistro, Le Chardenoux des Prés. First and foremost, I should like
to thank my entire team of waiters and cooks for their daily commitment, chefs
Aude Rambour, Chloé Monchalin and Olivier Palazzo for their creativity and their
professionalism. Thanks to Thomas Dhellemmes and Garlone Bardel for their mouth-
watering photographs and for their intuitive understanding of each project.
Thanks also to Arthur Delloye for his wonderful photography that captures
so quintessentially the atmosphere of this restaurant.
Another big thank you to Oliver Prodhon, the restaurant manager, for his support
and his valuable overview of our wonderful restaurant business.
And to David Van Kapelle, my loyal companion."

Cyril Lignac

———

All of Thomas Dhellemmes' team
warmly thank Cyril Lignac's team
for their generosity and devotion.

Le Chardenoux des Prés
27, rue du Dragon, 75006 Paris
Tel: 01 45 48 29 68

www.restaurantlechardenouxdespres.com

———

Restaurant's photography on page 2: © Yann Deret

cuisine attitude
BY CYRIL LIGNAC

La cuisine de mon Bistrot
The Cuisine Attitude cooking school
invites you to try bistrot cuisine sessions !

WWW . CUISINEATTITUDE .COM

10, cité Dupetit Thouars, 75003 Paris - Tél. +33 (0)1 49 96 00 50 - Contact : ecole@cuisineattitude.com

Open Tuesday to Saturday

First published by
© 2012 Hachette Livre (Hachette Pratique), Paris.
Original title: *Le Chardenoux des prés, La cuisine de mon bistrot*
Graphic designer: Nadine Ziadé Postel (npeg.fr)
Revisor: Stéphan Lagorce

© 2013 Octopus.
Translation: Kate Rignell
Reviser: Jinni Lyons
Graphic designer: Nadine Ziadé Postel (npeg.fr)

January 2013
23.1569.5
ISBN: 978.2.01.231569.3

Printed in Spain by Grafica Estellas.